Holistic Quality

Managing, Restructuring, and Empowering Schools

The Practicing Administrator's Leadership Series
Jerry J. Herman and Janice L. Herman, Editors

**ROADMAPS
TO SUCCESS**

Other Titles in the Series Include:

The Practicing Administrator's Leadership Series
Jerry J. Herman and Janice L. Herman, Editors

ROADMAPS TO SUCCESS

Holistic Quality

Managing, Restructuring, and Empowering Schools

Jerry J. Herman

CORWIN PRESS, INC.
A Sage Publications Company
Newbury Park, California

For information address:

Corwin Press, Inc.
A Sage Publications Company
2455 Teller Road
Newbury Park, California 91320

SAGE Publications Ltd.
6 Bonhill Street
London EC2A 4PU
United Kingdom

SAGE Publications India Pvt. Ltd.
M-32 Market
Greater Kailash I
New Delhi 110 048 India

Printed in the United States of America

Library of Congress Cataloging-in-Publication Data

Herman, Jerry, 1930–
    Holistic quality : managing, restructuring, and empowering schools
/ Jerry J. Herman.
        p. cm. — (Roadmaps to success)
    Includes bibliographical references.
    ISBN 0-8039-6053-0
    1. School management and organization—United States. 2. Teacher
participation in administration—United States. 3. Total quality
management—United States. 4. Educational planning—United States.
I. Title. II. Series.
LB2806.H457 1992
371.2'00973—dc20   92–38984

93 94 95 96 10   9   8   7   6   5   4   3   2   1

Corwin Press Production Editor: Marie Louise Penchoen

Contents

    • Quality Management Defined • Planning to
    Implement Quality Management • Requirements
    for the Management of QM • Monitoring,
    Collecting, Evaluating, and Providing Feedback
    Related to the Effectiveness of QM •
    Theory-to-Practice Example • Final Words

    • Effective Schools Research • Using the
    Correlates as Strategic Goals • Designing Specific
    Objectives and Action Programs to Achieve the
    Strategic Goals • Designing, Collecting, and
    Evaluating Effectiveness Data Related to the
    Strategic Goals • An Abbreviated Theory-to-
    Practice School-related Example • Final Words

Preface

Many events in the industrial, university, and governmental sectors have an impact on the structures, strategies, and tactics utilized by the school districts of the United States of America. The latest of these impacting events is Total Quality Management (TQM), sometimes referred to simply as Quality or Quality Management (QM). Although this movement originated in Japan based on the work of Dr. W. Edwards Deming following the rebuilding of Japanese industry after World War II, it is currently receiving much added attention from industries, businesses, universities, and government groups. Interest in QM is increasing in many school districts, and QM is receiving a great deal of attention from the American Association of School Administrators and other professional educational groups.

The reason for the increased interest in QM is easily traced to the following factors: (1) in the 1990s numerous books and articles about QM have been written, and journals such as *Quality Digest* and *Quality Progress* are providing a consistent flow of new information about the quality movement in both the manufacturing and service fields; (2) many large and small companies are opting for their tailor-made approach to QM;

(3) in 1991, the Congress of the United States established the Malcomb Baldridge National Quality Award to provide visibility for the outstanding work done by two companies each year in the three categories of manufacturing, service, and small business; and (4) on October 10, 1992, the Rochester Institute of Technology and *USA Today* announced the Quality Cup winners who were selected from over 2,000 organizations that requested applications. The five categories from which the winners were selected included large manufacturing firms, service firms, nonprofit institutions, governmental agencies, and businesses with fewer than 500 employees.

With all this publicity, and with many school board members serving in the business and industrial sectors, general community members reading about the quality movement, and educators looking for a variety of aids to restructure schools in their desire to produce higher-quality products, QM assuredly will affect the schools on a broader basis. The near future will see increased use of QM in schools.

Because the QM movement can be very important in making our schools better, it is essential to determine how QM can fit with the variety of other relatively new restructuring ideas that have become popular within the past decade. It is even more important to determine whether or not the QM movement can be combined with the structures and processes now in place in many school districts. If QM can be integrated into a holistic approach to quality improvement with the structures and processes of (1) effective schools, (2) strategic and tactical planning, and (3) the empowerment movement called School-based (Site-based) Management (SBM), it is possible to develop a very pragmatic, workable, affordable, efficient, and effective approach to the restructuring and quality improvement of our schools.

The purpose of this book is to present an integrated approach to *Holistic Quality* management by combining the structures and processes used in the past with QM and by empowering the stakeholders and customers to assist in developing this Holistic Quality approach to improving schools. Through integration of the key ideas of the various programs currently having an impact on schools, a systems approach can be developed and utilized in a very pragmatic way to assist in quality improvement. This approach will avoid fragmentation and a "bandwagon" approach to quality management and achievement in schools.

JERRY J. HERMAN

About the Author

Jerry J. Herman is currently a Professor and the Area Head for Administration and Educational Leadership at the University of Alabama. During his career, he has distinguished himself in numerous university and public school administrative posts. He served as Professor of Educational Administration at Iowa State University, Western Kentucky University, and Cleveland State University. He also served as Adjunct Professor of Educational Leadership, while he was a superintendent of schools, for Northern Michigan University, Eastern Michigan University, Michigan State University, and the University of Michigan.

His public school experiences include teaching elementary, junior high, senior high, and junior college courses. He also has taught numerous management and leadership courses at the graduate level. He has served as a principal, an elementary curriculum director, a secondary curriculum director, a director of district level research, an assistant superintendent of instruction, and a superintendent of schools for approximately 20 years in districts in Michigan and New York.

He has served as a consultant to industry, school districts, universities, and foundations; and he has served on many national committees. He is widely published, having authored a dozen books on various management and leadership topics; and he has published well over 125 articles on management and leadership in a wide variety of national journals. In addition, he has received numerous national honors for his leadership. Most important, he writes about matters that he has put into practice during his various personal administrative leadership positions.

Quality Management: Modifying It for School Use

This chapter (1) defines Quality Management, (2) discusses the planning that must precede the changes required prior to implementing QM in schools, (3) discusses the requirements of managing the QM program once it has been implemented, (4) emphasizes the monitoring and feedback components required, (5) provides a theory-to-practice example, and (6) presents final words.

Quality Management Defined

Various authors have their own definitions for Total Quality Management, Quality Process, Quality, or any of the variety of other terms used to demonstrate this movement. Since there is no single agreed-upon definition, the one used in this book includes three elements:

- *Philosophy:* Quality Management believes in providing an ever-improving quality of products and services to the organization's customers, and also believes in soliciting and utilizing customer feedback to develop specifications of the quality levels for both products and services to be strived for and achieved by those managing the QM operation in the school district and/or in its component school buildings.

- *Goal:* Each product and service delivered to customers, and all milestones leading to the delivery of each product or service, will be of the highest quality.
- *Process:* Feedback from all stakeholders is solicited and utilized to assist in achieving continuing quality improvements. It is a process that empowers and trains employees within a systems structure to use their talents at each value-added step of the development of a product or service. Also, it is done in a manner that causes customer satisfaction with the products and services the school district or its component schools deliver.

Planning to Implement Quality Management

To successfully implement and maintain Quality Management in a school district or its schools, a comprehensive planning model must be devised and used. The requirements that must be incorporated when designing a QM model follow.

The first requirement is to educate the key decision makers about QM and then to obtain a positive go-ahead signal from the board of education, school administration, and a critical mass of stakeholders. Only as key decision makers possess a good understanding of what is involved in QM and of its potential positive results can ownership be broadened to the degree necessary to predict successful implementation.

A second requirement is to conduct a comprehensive needs assessment. This needs assessment should involve the employees, the internal student customers, and the external community customers. Customers are those individuals and groups that must perceive the products and services of the schools as being of high quality. A needs assessment of each of these categories involves collecting significant hard data (such as student achievement scores) and significant soft data (such as opinion and/or attitude surveys). A comprehensive needs assessment also directs the investigation to three levels of *needs* (gaps between *what is* and *what should be* or *what could be*). The three levels consist of *mega* needs (those that the schools share with society), *macro* needs (those that involve the entire school district), and *micro* needs (those that involve individual schools or some other subelement of a school or school district).

Third, once a comprehensive needs assessment has been completed, it is important that *strategic goals* be established for each of the mega, macro, and micro categories of needs. These strategic goals can then be used by the planners to develop the fourth requirement—*quality specifications* (specific measurable objectives) for each of the services and products to be delivered by the school district and its constituent schools.

Fifth, the planning stakeholders have developed the quality specifications, and those responsible for *tactical planning* have to develop the means, ways, or programs designed to achieve the quality specifications agreed upon by the strategic planning stakeholders. This tactical planning stage of implementation of QM involves deciding on the specific programs to be attempted in order to achieve the desired quality specifications and the strategic goals that are to be addressed. This stage of planning includes (1) deciding on each task to be completed and the chronological sequence for completion of each task to be included as a part of each action program; (2) determining which person or group is responsible for completing each task; (3) establishing timelines for completion of each task; and (4) determining the resource allocations to be provided for the accomplishment of each task.

The sixth requirement is an ongoing one: Once the action plan is initiated, *formative evaluative data* are collected and analyzed for use in making decisions; and once the action program is completed, *summative data* are collected to determine the degree to which the program assisted in reaching the qualitative level of results spelled out in the initial quality specifications.

Requirements for the Management of QM

With the tactical plans completed, those who are to manage the QM action plans take over the responsibility for the degree of success to be achieved by the QM structure and processes. Although creating a climate conducive to the introduction of QM is vital to getting correctly started with this method of restructuring, it is every bit as important that those who are to manage QM on an ongoing basis fulfill the promise of Quality Management by making certain that each milestone and each subtask is completed in the highest possible quality manner.

Managers of the QM process must take the following actions:

- Instill a culture in all employees that creates and maintains an attitude of continual striving for improved quality in all products and services.
- Make every employee feel an integral part of the decision-making and delivery systems that collectively create a total organizational effort to achieve quality.
- Arrange for data collection and feedback to assist each employee and the entire organization in creating improved procedures that will lead to an ever-increasing quality of both the products and services delivered.

Monitoring, Collecting, Evaluating, and Providing Feedback Related to the Effectiveness of QM

Formative and summative evaluations are crucial if the continuing improvement in the quality of products and services is the oversight strategic goal of QM. Formative evaluative data provide important information at each step of the delivery system, and they can be used to determine whether or not the value-added targets are being met. Summative evaluative data provide information at the end of a predetermined time period of program implementation, and they can be used to modify, eliminate, or continue strengthening the programs put in place to meet the goal of continually improving products and services.

As an example of the use of formative data, an elementary school attempted to increase the reading achievement scores of students by initiating a whole-language approach in the elementary grades. The initial results were not promising. In investigating the procedures utilized in implementing the whole-language approach, the principal and teachers realized that inadequate staff development had been provided. Immediately, while the whole-language approach was in its infancy, the school instituted a comprehensive staff development program focused on a whole-language teaching approach.

As an example of the use of summative evaluative data, a secondary school attempted to reduce the dropout rate of its students by providing an in-house suspension program for potential dropouts who had disciplinary problems in school. Because there were no other intensive efforts to change attitudes, and alternate instructional programs were not attempted, the in-house suspension program became, simply, a holding pen for misbehaving potential dropouts. The summative evaluation data indicated that absolutely no improvement was evidenced in the student dropout rate. This evidence signaled a need to change what happened within the in-house suspension program or to drop the program and devise another, more successful program to reduce the student dropout rate.

Theory-to-Practice Example

For the last six years I have taught a graduate class in strategic and tactical planning. During these years I have asked for in-class, end-of-class, and end-of-course feedback from my student customers. By outlining the methods of instructional delivery utilized during year one compared to the methods used during year six, it is easy to determine the positive effects of *customer feedback*. In addition to changing delivery methods, the products of the students at each value-added stage have dramatically improved; and on a five-point scale, the students almost unanimously rate the course, the delivery methods, and the teacher with fives on all matters evaluated.

In year one, delivery consisted of a traditional sequence of students (1) hearing lectures, (2) reading the text, (3) reciting in class, and (4) passing exams. In year six, the delivery methods have dramatically changed. They include the following instructional methods:

- *Multi-media* presentations are made by the professor and the students, and some class activities are videotaped for review and critique.
- Students choose a *growth partner,* and these duos contact each other and meet between class sessions to get to know more about each other as individuals, to serve as mutual cheerleaders, and to share their thoughts about the topics discussed in class. Growth partners report on their communications at the beginning of each class session.
- At the end of each class session, a *debriefing session* of major learnings is conducted.
- Each student completes a *reflective journal* entry after each class session. The journal follows this format: (1) outline the major points gained from the class; (2) converse with persons in the field who are involved in the areas discussed in class, and list the major learnings gained from these discussions; (3) do substantial outside readings on the subject(s) discussed during the class period, and outline the major learnings from each source; and (4) after reviewing all of this information, write a narrative about final learnings, thoughts, and approaches the student would use when given responsibility for dealing with the area(s) discussed in class.
- Students choose groups of five to work through a *simulated strategic and tactical plan.* This simulation includes each step of a strategic and a tactical plan for their workplace or a hypothetical organization. This simulation continues throughout most class sessions.
- Two class sessions are spent *in the field,* where students conduct an external (outside their organization) and an

internal (within their organization) scanning of data to determine trends related to variables that could negatively or positively affect their strategic and tactical plans.

- Students work with their organization to develop a *detailed strategic and tactical plan*. This is a very practical and useful product.
- A *final exam* is required, but it is counted only as 10% of the course grade. *The questions for this final exam are derived from a series of pertinent questions submitted by each student.*

I only wish that I had solicited feedback in year one; I am certain that more positive instructional delivery changes will be made as I continue to receive valued customer feedback. The results of customer feedback have led to value-added products and services and a very high degree of customer satisfaction.

Final Words

Anyone in education today who is not concerned about the quality of the services and products delivered by individual schools and by school districts—or any leader in business, in industry, in any governmental unit, or in any social agency not concerned about the industry's services and products—must be imitating the ostrich with its head buried in the sand. The quest for quality by any organization is an admirable one, and the demand of customers for quality assurances of products and services is a most reasonable expectation.

Decision makers for a school district or a school building who initiate Quality Management that (1) utilizes the support of a critical mass of stakeholders and (2) uses a *mega, macro,* and *micro needs assessment* to determine the gaps or discrepancies between the quality of the products and/or the services desired and the quality currently being delivered and to establish goals and plans to achieve the quality specifications desired, are well on their way to leading their organizations to successful improvements.

However, the best goals and specifications will not result in successful implementation of QM without the implementation of tactical plans that spell out the answers to the questions of why? who? what? where? when? and how? It takes detailed planning to make QM work well, and it takes continuous formative data collection, feedback, and evaluation to provide a value-added approach to quality improvement. Finally, it takes periodic summative data collection, evaluation, and feedback to ensure the qualitative health of the organization and to ensure that its services and products are continuing to be the best that can be delivered at any measured point in time.

Effective Schools Research: Key to a Holistic Approach

This chapter (1) identifies the Effective Schools Correlates; (2) presents suggestions for the potential uses of the correlates as cornerstones for high-quality strategic goals; (3) discusses ideas for designing action programs based upon these strategic goals; (4) discusses the designing, collecting, and evaluating the impact and effectiveness data related to the strategic goals; (5) presents a theory-to-practice example; and (6) provides final words.

Research on effective schools is well into its third decade. Effective schools avoid things that do not work, and they capitalize on things that work well. They create a climate and culture in which all personnel are focused on effective learning for *all* students.

Effective Schools Research

Throughout the years of research, certain characteristics of effective schools have evolved. Most of these characteristics have been derived from statistically significant *correlative* research findings. Simply stated, a positive correlation result means that the characteristic(s) being assessed exists in schools that are effective; if the characteristics are absent or not present to a sufficient degree, the schools are judged to be ineffective. Correlative research findings are not considered as convincing as *cause and effect* research, wherein statistical proof exists that when a certain variable or item is introduced, the desired effect (result) will occur to a statistically significant degree.

In the area of education, correlative research findings are very helpful in determining directions that a school district and its schools should take to improve the education of the students in their charge. Over the past three decades, correlative research findings have indicated that the following characteristics are associated with schools judged to be effective.

- *Strong instructional leadership.* Effective principals are actively involved in student achievement monitoring, curriculum planning, staff development, and all instructional issues. A clear vision of what should be and a clarity of mission, goals, and objectives also exist.
- *A safe and orderly school climate conducive to learning.* Studies indicate that effective schools not only possess a safe and orderly climate, but also possess a climate of caring and high expectations for all students.
- *High teacher and administrator expectations of students.* These are exhibited by the format of classroom management, time spent on instructional tasks, and the expectation of mastery learning by each student. In other words, there exists a focus on instructional results.
- *High emphasis on the mastery of basic skills by all students in the areas of reading, writing, mathematics, and language arts.* Also, this emphasis may influence student achievement in other curricular areas. These are expected outcomes. Obviously, maximizing the instructional time spent by students on their academic tasks is also important to achieving mastery.

- *Regular and continuing feedback on the academic progress of each student.* These data are used by all teachers and all students, and they are distributed as a means of effective two-way communication with parents or guardians. Standardized norm-referenced tests are item analyzed, and criterion-referenced tests are used to determine whether or not each student can do exactly what is expected. The data from both types of tests are disaggregated to determine the achievement patterns that may differ among the sexes, socioeconomic levels, students at risk, or any other subcategorizations, which will assure that the individual student's achievement will not be masked by some generalized average score. Each child or youth is a very important product, and each must achieve well in school in order to become a productive future citizen.

- *Parent and community involvement.* Parents and community members and organizations have to be supportive of the vision, mission, goals, and procedures of the schools if schools are to be effective. If parents, community leaders, and groups are not supportive, the chances of successful student achievement and employee effectiveness will probably diminish.

Using the Correlates as Strategic Goals

A strategic goal states in general terms what result is desired. Each goal will have to be narrowed to specific objectives as well as tactical (action) plans to develop the means (hows) to achieve the goal and objectives. At this juncture, the Effective Schools Correlates can be listed as strategic goals:

- Strong instructional leadership will be provided by teachers and administrators.
- Schools will be kept safe, and an orderly climate will be maintained.
- Teachers and administrators will hold high expectations for all students' achievement.

- Teachers and administrators will place much emphasis on quality instruction to achieve student mastery of basic skills.
- Monitoring of students' achievement levels and provision of feedback will be continuous.
- Parents and community stakeholders will be involved in making decisions designed to create more effective schools.

Designing Specific Objectives and Action Programs to Achieve the Strategic Goals

To illustrate the development of specific objectives and action programs to achieve the strategic goals, two examples are provided. The two strategic goals selected are (1) schools will be kept safe, and an orderly climate will be maintained; and (2) parents and community stakeholders will be involved in making decisions designed to create more effective schools.

Strategic Goal 1: Schools Will Be Kept Safe, and an Orderly Climate Will Be Maintained

Objective 1: Negative outside forces and individuals will *never* be permitted within the school buildings. This safe climate objective has a 100% qualifier. The *never* indicator names the specific level to be used as the qualitative measurement.

Action Plan: Plainclothes police will be hired to monitor the halls and observe the entrances and exits in those schools that have a history of problems with outside negative forces invading the school buildings during the instructional day.

Objective 2: Schools shall decrease the number of health and safety problems by a minimum of 50% each school year. This will maximize the time that students spend on instructional tasks.

Action Plan: Each school shall have a representative health and safety committee, and written monthly reports of any health or safety problem shall be sent to the principal and to the central administration. Whenever possible, recommendations to solve the problem shall be suggested by the building's health and safety committee.

Objective 3: The interruption of student instructional time in each school shall be limited to less than five minutes per school day.

Action Plan 1: A student behavior guide shall be developed by a committee of parents, students, teachers, and administrators; and this guide shall be provided, yearly, to each student and each parent or guardian. This guide shall be used as a management tool to assess and enforce the agreed-upon behavior standards.

Action Plan 2: Visitors will be permitted in the classrooms only if they have received prior permission from the principal and the teacher agrees to the time of the classroom visit.

Action Plan 3: The intercom system will be used only prior to the beginning of classes or at the end of the school day, prior to student dismissal.

Strategic Goal 2: Parents and Community Stakeholders Will Be Involved in Making Decisions Designed to Create More Effective Schools

Objective 1: Any major change in instructional or management procedures by the school district or by the individual school building shall be reviewed by parents and community stakeholders, and feedback will be solicited from them before any major change is implemented. The measurement is indicated by the statement that *any major change in instructional management* is to be shared.

Action Plan 1: Any major change contemplated in the areas of instruction or management shall be provided to the media prior to any implementation.

Action Plan 2: All parents shall be mailed an information sheet about a proposed change and the reasons why it is being contemplated.

Action Plan 3: A phone survey will be conducted with a stratified random sampling of community residents for the purpose of receiving feedback about the proposed change and to discover the degree of positive, neutral, or negative attitude toward the proposed change.

Action Plan 4: The superintendent of schools shall create a key communicators committee of 100 influential community members to assess and provide feedback about any major changes and to provide advice to the superintendent. This group will have quarterly scheduled meetings, and it will also meet any time a major change in instruction or management is being contemplated.

Action Plan 5: Each school building shall establish a school-based management council consisting of five parents, five nonparent citizens, five teachers, five students at the senior high level (if applicable), and the school's principal. Also, a central office administrator or supervisor shall be assigned as a liaison to each school building, but this functionary/facilitator will not possess a vote. This group shall be informed and asked for their thoughts prior to any significant change in instruction or management procedures before they are implemented.

Designing, Collecting, and Evaluating Effectiveness Data Related to the Strategic Goals

It does little good to have admirable strategic goals, clearly worded measurable objectives, and well-intentioned tactical action plans if data are not collected, analyzed, and used to determine the degree to which the desired results have been met. Thus, it is important that, prior to implementing the action plans, an evaluation methodology is determined.

The strategic goal of providing regular and continuing feedback about each student's progress will be used as an example, and the example will also include the strategic goal of emphasis placed on mastery of the basic skills of reading and mathematics. An evaluation scheme might well include soft (attitudinal) data and hard (factual) data; this example will incorporate both types.

Students' Elementary School's Evaluation Structure

Students' Elementary School intends to make judgments about the effectiveness of its reading and mathematics instruction by the following procedures; both formative (in process) and summative (end of school year) evaluations shall be conducted.

1. The action programs (curriculum and delivery methods) for students involved in reading and mathematics learning opportunities shall be based upon the most recent research on the effectiveness of contents and delivery methods.
2. During the school year (*formative stage*) (1) student attitudes toward instruction shall be monitored by observation of the time spent on task; (2) student attitudes toward instruction shall be assessed by structured interviews; (3) parental and guardian attitudes toward their child's attitude and achievement in math and reading shall be monitored quarterly by conducting a random sample of homes through structured phone surveys; and (4) teacher-administered criterion-referenced tests shall be given to determine whether mastery has been achieved (with mastery defined as a minimum of 80% correct answers on the items tested).
3. At the completion of the school year (*summative stage*) (1) criterion-referenced testing (testing based on specific items that prove the student can apply the learnings) will be administered, and (2) norm-referenced national tests (which compare achievement with a nationally normed group of students on the same tests) in reading and mathematics will be administered.

Whether the tests are of the norm-referenced or the criterion-referenced type, they must be analyzed in detail to determine the effectiveness level of learning of all students, subgroups of students, and the individual student. Any deficiencies noted in student learning must be addressed by redesigning the curriculum offered, the delivery of instruction system utilized, or the means used to motivate students to learn the desired information and required skills. When dealing with the analysis of student achievement and the instructional program, it is suggested that educators believe that the occurrence of any student failing to achieve at a level that seems appropriate for that student be initially considered as a flaw in instruction. That is, barring a serious mental defect, any student can learn; but if instruction is not effective, it may cause a deficiency in the student's level of learning.

When the raw data have been collected on the summative criterion-referenced and norm-referenced tests, they must be micro-analyzed to make certain that no underachieving student is allowed to drop through the cracks because the data are not broken down into sufficient detail. At the very least, a comprehensive data analysis of both criterion-referenced and norm-referenced test data should include the following:

- The tests should be item analyzed to determine whether the item is important and whether it directly measures the instructional details provided. In other words, it is determined whether or not the individual test item has validity for the instructional program delivered and for the students who have done the learning. If the test item is not valid, it should be eliminated (by extrapolation) from the group of students' and the individual student's test results.

- Besides comparing the group of students' and each individual student's achievement results on norm-referenced tests, the local school district and local school should develop their own local norms in order to allow comparison of an individual student's achievement with that of others in the student's own school or with the school district's grade and agemates who have completed the same test.

- Whether the test is of the criterion-referenced or norm-referenced variety, the data should be disaggregated by sex, age, socioeconomic level, or any other important variables to determine whether there are trends that indicate a modified instructional procedure is required to do a better job with instructional content or delivery methods with certain subgroups of students or with individual students.

- Each student's test achievement results must be compared with the results achieved by that student during the summative testing of the previous year. It is important to realize that while a student may not have tested at the 50th percentile or at the student's grade level on the most recently administered test, this same student may have increased achievement level by 10% or gained two and one-half grade levels, even though she/he remains below the 50th percentile or below grade level in achievement.

The message is a simple one. Testing, whether it is of the norm-referenced or the criterion-referenced variety, is of no value unless the raw data are manipulated to obtain every drop of information upon which to make knowledgeable and effective decisions that will assist each child and the entire student population to become more effective in their levels of learning.

An Abbreviated Theory-to-Practice School-related Example

Before detailing an abbreviated practical example of a school using the Effective Schools Research, let us identify a model that will indicate the interconnections and supplemental details to assist in the implementation of the basic correlates of effective schools (see Table 2.1).

- Strong instructional leadership shall be provided by all teachers and by all administrators connected with the school.
- Continual monitoring of student achievement levels will be conducted, and the results will be used to make desired improvements in the instructional delivery systems.

Once the preferred future vision has been determined, a *mission statement* should be agreed upon by the stakeholders' planning group:

The mission of Successful Middle School is to provide quality instruction that will allow our students to achieve at high levels that, in turn, will enable them to be very successful when they enter senior high school. Parents and community members will be involved in assisting in achieving this mission.

When the vision and mission have been determined, the next planning step is that of stating *strategic goals*. Three of the most important goals developed for Successful Middle School include

- Students will regularly attend school, and they will arrive at school in a timely manner.
- Each student will achieve at a high level of academic achievement.
- Each student will achieve at a minimum of one year's level of achievement or at a greater than one year's level of achievement in all basic subjects for each year of attendance at Successful Middle School.

Once the strategic goals are determined, they should spell out the desired results of *what should be*. Once the what should be results have been determined, they can be compared to the current, or *what is*, level of achievement on the goal areas. The discrepancy or gap between the what should be and the what is levels determines the *needs* to be addressed. In other words, a need is the gap or discrepancy that exists between the what should be and the what is state of affairs in the school related to the strategic goals.

Once the strategic goals are developed, *specific measurable objectives* must be developed. Using the above strategic goals and the needs assessment data, the stakeholders' planning committee developed the following specific objectives:

> *Specific Objective 1:* By the end of the year, the student absentee and tardiness rates will be lessened by a minimum of 25% when compared to identical data from the previous school year.
>
> *Specific Objective 2:* As a group, student improvement will increase by a minimum of 5% over the past three years' pattern; within five years, there will be a decrease of a minimum of 30% in the number of individual students who are achieving below their grade level.

Once the specific objectives are determined, action programs must be developed. Action programs initiated by the stakeholders' planning committee at Successful Middle School related to Specific Objective 1 include (1) opening the schools before and after school for a latchkey program for working parents, (2) establishing a call to the home system every day for every student who is absent or tardy, and (3) providing a monthly assembly for the purpose of providing certificates to students who have had improved attendance records and for providing an even higher level of recognition for students who have had perfect attendance for the month and for the school year to date.

The stakeholders' committee developed the following action plans related to Specific Objective 2: (1) an after-school study program, which included a school-based study room proctored by volunteer teachers; (2) a telephone student assistance system staffed by teachers, administrators, and trained volunteers; and (3) a daily homework and testing procedure for each class.

The action programs detailed the answers to the following questions:

- Why is this tactic being implemented?
- Who is responsible for the achievement of each task to bring this program into operation?
- What specifically is to become part of this program?
- How will this program be implemented?
- When will this program be implemented?
- Where will this program be housed?
- What resources will be provided to implement this program?
- How will one determine if the results of this program meet the expectations?

Once the action plans are decided upon, the next task becomes one of collecting formative and summative data of both the hard and soft varieties. These data, then, can be used to decide whether or not the program attempted is at a satisfactory level, whether the program should be continued or eliminated, or whether there are some modifications to be made that will improve the program as it is implemented in the future.

Final Words

Schools exist for the primary purpose of producing productive future citizens. A productive citizen may be defined as one who produces more than she or he consumes. Productive citizens must become well educated, and the task of assisting students to become high-level achievers falls to those who are held responsible for providing a learning environment and an instructional delivery system that will accomplish the goal of delivering, after 12 or 13 years, high-achieving, productive graduates.

Effective Schools Research provides a series of findings from correlative research that will allow the local school district's decision makers to initiate practical and research-based actions to assist in improving their local schools. With the correlates in mind and with the will to improve, schools can become effective, and students can become high-achieving, productive members of adult society.

School-based Management: How It Fits With Quality Improvement

This chapter (1) defines School-based Management (SBM); (2) discusses the structure and processes related to SBM; (3) emphasizes the requirement to resolve possible decision-making authority and responsibility questions related to instruction, finance, personnel, policy, and governance matters that must be decided between individual schools and the central level of a school district; and (4) presents final words.

School-based Management, sometimes called Site-based Management, is a growing movement among school districts in the United States. It combines two current popular themes: *restructuring* and *empowering*.

Definitions

Restructuring refers to dramatic change in the structure and/or processes of an organization, compared to the traditional way of doing business. *Empowering* refers to a purposeful decision to allow power and accountability to flow from the traditional

source of power to individuals who previously were not provided with decision-making authority. Both of these themes
come into play in SBM.

School-based Management is an increasingly popular movement championed by innovators, change agents, legislatures,
school boards, teachers' unions, and individuals within school
districts to change the way school business has been tradition-
ally conducted. It represents a dramatic change in processes
and structure from the traditional way districts have been man-
aged. *School-based Management* reallocates and redistributes decision-making authority in many areas, from the central district
level to the individual school level. It involves representatives
of teachers, parents, and sometimes community members and
students in making decisions in some or all of the areas of
budget, personnel, instruction, policy, student services, and
governance.

SBM Structure and Processes

Unless the structure and processes are legislated, as is the
case in the Kentucky Reform Act of 1990, each school district's
decision makers who are responsible for planning SBM in their
district must decide on which stakeholders to involve in SBM.
In addition, they must negotiate which decisions and the degree to which final decision power are to be shared between the
central district level and the local school level.

Deciding on the Stakeholders to Involve in SBM

There are various ways of involving stakeholders in the planning and operation of a SBM approach. In all probability, it is
wise to assemble a SBM steering committee composed of the
representatives of the various stakeholder groups; the committee's membership should be small enough to accomplish the
tasks, yet large enough to be truly representative. Of course, to
really get large groups of stakeholders to claim ownership, the

steering committee should create a series of subcommittees to report data and make recommendations.

Once the decision to create a SBM steering committee and to allow it to create a series of subcommittees has been made, the question of the categories of membership must be addressed. The options include (1) the building principal, (2) teachers, (3) building-level classified employees, (4) a central office liaison, (5) parents, (6) community members, (7) business, industrial, civic, and other governmental unit representatives, and (8) students—usually restricted to those at the secondary schools. Let us analyze the importance of inclusion for each of these representatives.

1. *The building principal*, research demonstrates, is a crucial player in the qualitative level achieved by students and employees in the local school building. This individual is ultimately charged with implementing laws, school board policies, and the SBM committee's decisions. It is crucial that this person be intimately involved in the structure and processes of SBM.

2. *Teachers* definitely must be involved because they are the employees who deal directly with the students. In a large school it will be impossible to involve all teachers in the SBM steering committee. It is important to allow the teachers to select their representatives; the remainder of the teachers can receive invitations to serve on the various subcommittees that are created.

3. *Classified employees* include such employees as food service workers, custodians, aides, maintenance personnel, and transportation employees. Since many of these people live in the community, and since they are very important to the efficient and effective daily operation of the school, it is important to allow them to elect at least one representative to the SBM steering committee. Of course, many others can be included as subcommittee members.

4. A *central office liaison* may be included as a communications link between the central office and the school. If it

is decided to include a central office person as a liaison to the school's SBM committee, it should be made clear that this person serves in an ad hoc capacity and that the liaison's sole role is that of a communications link.

5. *Parents* are probably the single most interested group of individuals, outside of the school district's employees, who want the school to make the wisest decisions possible related to the education of their youngsters. Although some SBM committees do not include parents, it is very important that these positively motivated individuals be included in the SBM committee's membership. If there is an active PTA or PTO, band boosters' group, sports boosters' group, or any other supportive school-related group, some method for these groups to elect their best representatives to the SBM committee must be decided upon with the help of the groups themselves.

6. *Community members'* involvement in the SBM steering committee is a matter of determining how many stakeholders can be encompassed within a workably sized committee. Certainly, if they can be accommodated, it is wise to include community representation. If this would cause the committee to be unwieldy, then it is important to include them in subcommittees.

7. *Business, industrial, civic, and other governmental unit representatives'* involvement focuses on the same rationale as that for involvement of community members. If there are power groups, without whose support the SBM movement will fail, some strategy must be created to include their representatives. If this is not the case, they definitely should be found in the subcommittee structure.

8. *Students* and the quality of their education are the sole reason for the existence of school districts. They are the products, and they form the future citizenry who will become either productive or nonproductive members of our society. To enhance the quality of their education, they should be an important source of data. It is recommended that the student body, at least at the middle and secondary levels, elect representatives to the committee

and that the adults accept them as full participants in the SBM processes.

In actual practice, in practically every SBM situation, the building principal and the teachers are on the SBM committee. Next in frequency of inclusion are parent members. Only seldom are the other stakeholder categories directly involved in the SBM committee. It is crucial that the school district and the individual schools develop broad-based, positive ownership for SBM. Although each district, and perhaps each school, will have to make its own membership decisions, it is crucial that this broad ownership be achieved to maximize the probability of success for SBM.

Determining the Decision-making Authority and Responsibility

Once the SBM committee's membership has been decided upon, the planners must turn to the areas and degrees of decision-making authority and responsibility to be delegated to the school level, to be retained by the central level, or to be shared by the individual school and central levels. Determination must be made by the central office authorities and the school-level decision makers about which decisions related to instruction, budget, personnel, and policy can be made at each level and which decisions require collaborative input.

Final Words

School-based Management can be an effective restructuring method if carefully and properly implemented and maintained. It is clearly an evolutionary, not a revolutionary, process. It requires time to get it really right. It should not be attempted if there is no desire by the traditional decision makers to allow nontraditional decision makers to become a part of the decision-making process for the children and residents at the school level. It also should not be attempted if the legally elected or appointed school board of education members, the superintendent, and the school district's administrators are not desirous of a collaborative approach to decision making and planning.

However, if there is a belief that those closest to the delivery of education to children can make valued, effective, and efficient judgments that will benefit students. School-based Management offers an opportunity to develop broad-based ownership and collective decision making, which has the potential to improve what happens at the local school building level and in the school districts of this nation.

Strategic and Tactical Planning: Integral to Success

This chapter (1) defines strategic and tactical planning, (2) provides reasons for school districts to conduct systematic planning, (3) presents a theory-to-practice example, and (4) provides final words.

Once the local school board, the superintendent, or other decision makers decide that formalized planning is required, they must choose their planning partners and their methodologies. Just as important is the selection of planners who can think and act strategically and tactically.

It is recommended that the district's prime decision makers create a strategic planning committee composed of a wide variety of stakeholders, such as teachers, principals, central office administrators, parents, students, and community members. This broad stakeholder representation, along with comprehensive and continuous two-way communication about what is to be accomplished and how it is to be accomplished with all stakeholders within the school district, will maximize the probability of broad-based understanding, support, and ownership of the structure, goals, and processes. Once the committee membership is determined and its written charge has been distributed, an initial set of orientation and training meetings should be held. At these meetings stress should be placed on (1) the definitions of strategic and tactical planning, (2) the reasons for conducting this planning, (3) the means of communicating to noncommittee stakeholders, (4) the methods of team building and collaborative decision making, and (5) the detailed steps of the planning processes.

Strategic and Tactical Planning Definitions

Strategic planning is long-term planning to achieve the preferred future vision for the organization and its component parts, activities, and programs. The key word is *vision*. Also, strategic planning focuses on the desired results, or the *whats* of achievement. Without a vision, the planning merely becomes long term; and since the desired ultimate results are not identified, two things may happen: (1) the planners and the managers of the educational enterprise may do an excellent job on relatively unimportant matters when compared to the overall scheme of things; or (2) they may arrive at a results destination by chance that has nothing to do with the destination at which they should have arrived. In the latter case they would be like a driver who was required to reach Chicago, but neither secured a road map nor planned the trip carefully—and who ended up in Detroit without realizing that the desired destination had been completely missed.

In contrast, *tactical planning* focuses on the means or *hows* of achieving the desired strategic *whats* (goals or results). This is the planning that deals with the details of operation. In all probability, at this stage of planning it is wise to eliminate the nonemployee stakeholders, unless they have specific helpful expertise. However, once the nonemployee stakeholders complete their strategic planning activities and provide them to the tactical planners, the nonemployee stakeholders should still be presented with periodic updates on the progress of the tactical plans and the results achieved related to the strategic goals.

The Reasons for Systematic Planning

Once the stakeholders clearly understand the terms *strategic* and *tactical* planning, they must be presented with, and buy into, the reasons for doing this comprehensive and long-term planning. It should be explained that the basic reasons for doing strategic and tactical planning (versus the immediate, day-to-day, year-to-year traditional planning done solely by the administrative staff) are as follows:

- We desire to involve a wide variety of stakeholders in the school district's planning in order to acquire broad-based support for and ownership of the programs, services, and product quality tendered by the school district and its individual schools.
- Committee members can generate a critical mass of support and ownership from the employees and community at large by communicating and selling the vision and the planning activities.
- Collectively, we must determine the preferred future vision of what we desire the school district to look like at some future point. This includes the results that we wish to witness in terms of services and products.
- Once the committee has determined the desired results, which will indicate that the preferred future vision has been reached, the committee members can compare those desired results to the results being currently achieved. This component of *what is* to *what should be* or *what could be* identifies the needs to be met. A *need* is a gap or discrepancy between what exists and what is desired in terms of results. Finally, once the needs are identified, the tactical planners can develop specific action plans designed to achieve the desired results, which

will ultimately indicate that the preferred future vision has been reached.

An Abbreviated Theory-to-Practice School-related Example

The hypothetical Desirable School District's planners have reached consensus, due to their collaborative planning approach, on the following points.

Strategic Planners' Agreements

A *vision* that includes student service to the community (mega level), a competent and successful group of employees (macro level), and individual schools that possess a high-quality school climate (micro level).

Beliefs that include the realization that all children can learn and that a wide variety of stakeholders have to become an integral part of the school district's decision-making processes.

Internal and external scanning activities that collect trendlines on such areas as student achievement, demographics, finance, and attitudes of students, employees, parents, and community residents and groups.

CSFs (Critical Success Factors) identification, which include high-achieving students, general public support, and a highly productive group of certified and classified employees.

Strategic goals that include decreasing the high schools' student dropout rates and improving the academic achievement of students who are identified as being at risk.

A *SWOT (strengths, weaknesses, opportunities, and threats) analysis* that discovered, among many other things, that (1) there was an aging population (both threat and opportunity), (2) there was support by other governmental units (strength), (3) the local teachers' union was considering a strike (threat), and (4) student test scores were unsatisfactory in the area of reading (weakness).

Specific, measurable objectives such as the one stating that the percentage of high school student dropouts will be reduced by a minimum of 50% within five years. Note that this step may be passed on by the stakeholders' strategic planning committee to the tactical planners.

A *recycling plan*, put into place in case changes caused unanticipated developments that were related to the trends, CSFs, beliefs, and values or data from the SWOT analysis changed significantly enough to cause the strategic planners to modify the vision, mission, or strategic goals.

Tactical Planners' Decisions

Decision rules were identified to prioritize the strategic goals and objectives, since they were too numerous to deal with in their entirety in the immediate future. Only three rules were selected: Is it doable? Is it affordable? Is it meaningful?

By *brainstorming*, with the use of formal rules, the strategic planners listed 85 potential alternative plans to solve the need to improve students' reading test scores.

A *force-field analysis* was applied, and the planners discovered that the action plan to use student tutors after school had, among other supporting and constraining factors, the supporting factor of the research on peer learning and the constraining factor that the parents and community residents were strongly against this approach because they felt the teachers should be responsible for all instruction.

A *cost/benefit analysis* indicated that the cost was insignificant for this approach but the loss of parental and community support was very great. However, the potential benefit to students and to their achievement levels in reading were high enough that the risk was taken, and a parental and community education informational and selling program was immediately begun in the hopes of eliminating the negativism.

The *best alternative* of all those investigated was determined to be the after-school student tutoring program.

The *resource allocation and action planning* activities first steps included assigning a specific teacher as coordinator and monitor of the after-school program and soliciting volunteer after-school student tutors.

Activities were returned to the strategic planners, and recycling activities were conducted. The results achieved by the action plans were shared with the stakeholders' strategic planning committee. Also, the formative and summative data were collected, analyzed, and evaluated; and decisions were made to continue the successful action programs, modify those that could be improved, and eliminate those that did not provide the expected positive impact results.

Celebrations took place for successes, and work began on the next set of action programs designed to achieve the specific objectives, strategic goals, and the preferred future vision of the school district and its component parts. *It is very important to take time to celebrate and publicize success, to admit failures, and to try again to continuously reach for the preferred future vision.*

Final Words

In any organization, including school districts, planning is a necessity if an effective and efficient operation is to take place. If one knows the destination to be reached (vision) and the roads to travel (action plans) to get to that destination in a timely, qualitative, and efficient manner; then productivity, success, a feeling of ownership, and celebration will result.

Integrating the Models
for Holistic Quality

This chapter (1) presents a view of a school-related quality approach that integrates the key elements of Quality Management (QM), Effective Schools, School-based Management (SBM), and strategic and tactical planning into a holistic and practical approach that can be used by school districts and by individual schools to improve the quality of their products and services; (2) offers a matrix model that illustrates the integrating factors of this approach; (3) discusses advantages and cautions related to this Holistic Quality approach to school improvement; (4) presents a practical school-related example; and (5) provides final words.

Regardless of which of the approaches to improvement is chosen—QM, SBM, Effective Schools, or strategic and tactical planning—change is involved. Whether that change becomes only cosmetic or whether it becomes true systemic transformational change, and whether it becomes a short-term or a long-term change, depends on many variables, such as ownership by a critical mass of believers, adequate temporal and human resources, and a long view aimed at achieving a vision of what should be. Systemic change has to focus on two organizational aspects: (1) the restructuring must *simultaneously focus* on the development and *interrelationships of all the main components* of the system, and (2) the restructuring must focus on *structure, process, and culture* simultaneously.

If a school district or an individual school is to change transformationally and systemically, and if the change is to create a culture that promotes dramatic changes in existing structures, processes, and attitudes, the likelihood of success is much greater if the separate approaches are unified and blended into one coordinated and complementary approach to transformational change and to a new systemic organizational culture.

It would be wise for the school district's or individual school's decision makers to assess their organization's readiness for change prior to attempting the individual change procedures of SBM, QM, Effective Schools, or strategic and tactical planning. Certainly, if the decision makers are going to attempt transformational change, which involves the integration of the individual change programs into one holistic and systemic change structure and process, they should always begin by assessing the organization's (which means the employees' and other stakeholders') readiness for such a change effort. By so doing, they can capitalize on areas of support and work to overcome areas of resistance. A simple way of doing a quick readiness for change analysis is to utilize a change readiness questionnaire, similar to the one presented in Figure 5.1.

Once the decision makers feel that the organization is sufficiently ready to attempt systemic, transformational change, they can address the task of integrating the various programs of QM, SBM, Effective Schools, and strategic and tactical planning into a holistic structure to achieve true systemic change. A simple model, like that presented in Figure 5.2, explains how QM, SBM, and Effective Schools fit within the concepts of strategic and tactical planning. Note that to create a preferred future vision for a school district or individual school, it is suggested that a stakeholders' School-based Management council be utilized. Next, the model suggests that strategic goals can be determined by using the Effective School Correlates in combination with an assessment of needs that have been garnered from conducting an internal and external scanning exercise. Finally, it is suggested that tactical plans (the how-to-do-its) utilize Total Quality Management procedures to achieve the strategic goals, and to achieve quality products, quality services, and satisfied internal and external school district or individual school customers.

Designing a Holistic Approach to Systemic Transformational Change

Reviewing the key concepts of QM, SBM, Effective Schools, and strategic and tactical planning, we find that a complementary blending of these concepts will allow the development of a holistic approach to positive systemic and transformational change in schools. The key concepts to be incorporated for QM, Effective Schools, and SBM are displayed as Figure 5.3, while the total array of key concepts, including those for strategic and tactical planning, are displayed as Figure 5.4.

Finally, the Holistic Matrix displayed as Figure 5.5 shows that, using the strategic and tactical planning concepts as the basic structure, it is possible, and profitable, to combine the concepts of QM, SBM, and Effective Schools with the planning concepts. It is also clear that each step of the strategic and tactical planning structure can accommodate the concepts of QM, SBM, and Effective Schools. Although some steps in the planning structures have stronger implications than others for the integration of QM, SBM, and Effective Schools into a holistic approach, it is clear that strong evidence exists in the commonality of the concepts of

- Empowered stakeholders
- Needs assessment
- Strategic goals
- Strategic objectives
- Action programs

- Data collection and feedback
- Planning
- Strong leadership
- Collaborative decision making
- Climate conducive to support

(Text continued on p. 43.)

Directions: Circle the number that most clearly identifies your attitude toward the statements listed.

strongly disagree (1)	disagree (2)	agree (3)	strongly agree (4)

1. My school (school district) has a clear *vision* of what should be in the future, and I agree with it.	1 2 3 4
2. My school (school district) has a clear idea of the needs (gaps) that exist between the vision of what *should be* and the current *what is* state, and I am informed about those needs.	1 2 3 4
3. Internal and external forces are pressuring for change in my school (school district).	1 2 3 4
4. I believe that the changes required are so great that they should transform my school's structures and processes into something drastically different for the future.	1 2 3 4
5. My school's (school district's) administrators, teachers, parents, and other interested parties are constantly looking for ways to improve.	1 2 3 4
6. My school (school district) believes in continuous planning about ways to improve.	1 2 3 4
7. My school (school district) collects information about the impact results of our programs and our efforts related to students, employees, and instruction.	1 2 3 4
8. My school (school district) expends money to train those who are managing new approaches or who are learning about innovations that may improve the schools.	1 2 3 4
9. My school (school district) gives everyone credit for successes achieved, and every success is publicly celebrated.	1 2 3 4
10. My school (school district) looks toward the future with positive visions, and it provides continuing plans for improvement of all its products and services.	1 2 3 4

Total Readiness Score: _____

Figure 5.1. An Organization's Readiness for Change Questionnaire

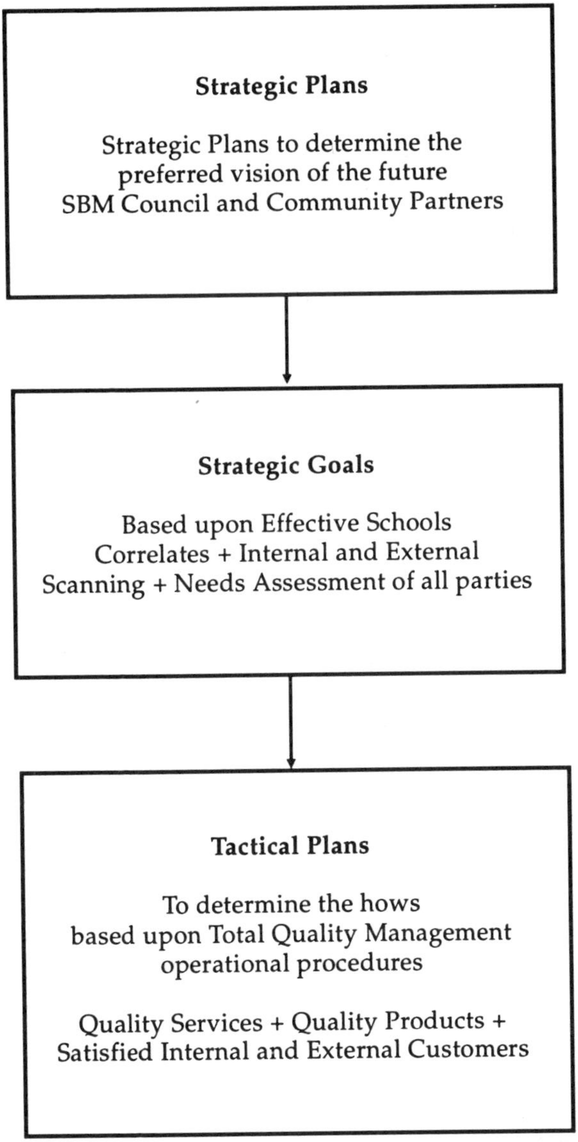

Figure 5.2. Tying QM, Effective Schools Research, Strategic Planning, School-based Management, and School-Community Partnerships Together in a Large, Inner-city School District

Quality Management

1. Vision of continually improving quality
2. Quality goals
3. Value-added concept of quality at each juncture
4. Quality results in products and services
5. Empowers stakeholders
6. Planning is continuous
7. Data collection and feedback
8. Customer satisfaction

Effective Schools

1. Vision of what should be (preferred future vision)
2. Strong instructional leadership
3. Safe and orderly climate conducive to learning
4. High expectations for achievement
5. Emphasis on mastery of basic skills
6. Regular and continuous feedback on academic progress
7. Parent and community involvement

School-based Management

1. Authority and accountability shifted to school site level
   (empowerment shift)
2. Collaborative decision making is the process used
3. Stakeholders are involved in school site decision making
4. A supportive climate exists

Figure 5.3. Key Planning Concepts

PLANNING STEPS

Strategic Plan

A. Vision
B. Beliefs and values
C. External and internal scanning
D. Critical success factors
E. Needs assessment
F. Mission
G. SWOT analysis
H. Strategic goals
I. Specific objectives for goals
J. Evaluate and recycle

Tactical Plan

K. Decision rules to determine priorities
L. Action plans
  (a) Brainstorm
  (b) Force-field Analysis
  (c) Cost/benefit Analysis
  (d) Select best alternative
  (e) Allocate resources and operate plans
M. Evaluate and recycle

KEY CONCEPTS

Quality Management
1. Vision
2. Goals
3. Empowerment
4. Continuous planning
5. Data collection and feedback
6. Value added at each juncture
7. Quality results (services and products)
8. Customer satisfaction

Effective Schools

1. Vision of preferred future
2. Instructional leadership
3. Parent and community involvement
4. Conducive climate
5. Emphasis on basic skills
6. Data collection and feedback
7. Mastery

School-based Management

1. Empowerment to the school site
2. Stakeholders' involvement in decision making
3. Collaborative decision making
4. Conducive support climate

Figure 5.4. Interface Between Planning Steps and Key Concepts

Directions: Place a large X when the characteristic is an absolute, and place a small x when the characteristic is applicable but not absolute.

Key Characteristics	SBM	QM	Eff Schs	Strat & Tact Planning
Strategic and Tactical Planning:				
1. Vision	x	x	x	X
2. Empowered stakeholders	X	X	X	X
3. Needs assessment	X	X	X	X
4. Goals	X	X	X	X
5. Objectives	X	X	X	X
6. Action programs	X	X	X	X
7. Data collection and feedback	X	X	X	X
8. Recycling	X	X	X	X
Quality Management:				
1. Quality service results	x	X	x	x
2. Quality products results	x	X	X	X
3. Value added at each juncture	x	X	x	x
4. Empowered stakeholders	X	X	X	X
5. Data collection and feedback	X	X	X	X
6. Customer satisfaction	x	X	x	x
7. Planning	X	X	X	X
Effective Schools:				
1. Strong leadership	X	X	X	X
2. Safe and orderly climate	x	x	X	x
3. High achievement expectations	x	X	X	X
4. Mastery	x	x	X	x
5. Data collection and feedback	X	X	X	X
6. Parents and community involved	X	x	X	X
School-based Management:				
1. Site level decision making	X	X	X	x
2. Empowered stakeholders	X	X	X	X
3. Collaborative decision making	X	X	X	X
4. Conducive support climate	X	X	X	X

Figure 5.5. Holistic Matrix for Systemic Transformational Change

With all this commonality, it should be clear that it makes great sense to plan as a holistic structure, rather than taking each of the five currently popular restructuring ideas—strategic planning, tactical planning, Effective Schools Research, Quality Management, and School-based Management—as independent methodologies to attempt school improvement. In fact, if more than one of these current restructuring efforts are attempted in the same school district or same school building, without being integrated into a single approach effort, conflict between or among the various restructuring methods could result in much damage. Also, if the initial efforts at restructuring are unsuccessful because of the lack of coordination between or among the various methods, it will be a very long time before stakeholders will be willing to accept another restructuring approach or to put their efforts into any change strategy.

The design of this integrated approach to school improvement and systemic transformational change will be illustrated in an abbreviated school-related example. Before providing this integrated approach example, however, it is important to list the advantages and cautions related to this comprehensive approach to restructuring schools.

Advantages and Cautions Related to a Holistic Quality Approach to School Improvement

There are several advantages related to a holistic quality approach to school improvement. (1) A holistic quality approach will avoid an attempt to jump on the bandwagon for every restructuring idea that is recommended. (2) It will avoid overlap and conflict among the various restructuring programs being attempted. (3) It will unify all individual and organizational efforts focused on a clear vision, goals, objectives, and series of action programs. (4) Employees and other stakeholders will understand that a well-planned, holistic approach to school improvement is being attempted by the school district and its constituent schools, and they will also realize what will remain in a stabilized condition and what will be changed.

(5) Change will take place on the basis of data collection, analysis, feedback, and recycling activities.

Although there are many advantages to a holistic quality approach to school improvement, there are some cautions that must be stressed. The major cautions include the following. (1) Causing holistic transformational and systemic change is much more complicated than merely integrating a single restructuring idea into an existing operational structure. (2) Implementing a holistic transformational and systemic change is a long-term, working- and thinking-intensive activity, and many individuals may not be up to this comprehensive challenge. (3) A holistic transformational and systemic change is a continuing, never-ending process, and the quest for continual quality improvement may be difficult to maintain as individuals change, as new people enter the employment of the school district, and as additional promising restructuring ideas have to be integrated into this holistic approach to transformational and systemic change.

An Abbreviated Theory-to-Practice
School-related Example

The following example uses the hypothetical Effective School District and the integrated matrix, as well as the details from chapters 1 through 4, to show how this holistic approach could be used in a school district. Of course, similar considerations would apply to an individual school's integrated approach to systemic transformational change.

Effective School District Example

The school board and superintendent of schools of Effective School District decided to organize a stakeholders' committee that would be oriented to the techniques used by strategic and tactical planners, and then to utilize these planning techniques to arrive at a holistic approach to restructuring. Also, the committee members were provided with information and training in the restructuring programs entitled (1) Quality Management, (2) School-based Management, and (3) Effective Schools. Finally, the stakeholders' committee, which was composed of teachers, principals, central office administrators, parents, students, and community representatives, was asked to complete a plan to utilize the key concepts of all these programs to arrive at a single structure, with related processes, for use in the Effective School District. The stakeholders' committee was also permitted to form subcommittees, involving other representative members, to assist in the work to be done in creating a holistic restructuring process.

The results of the stakeholders' committee's work are abbreviated below. These results were obtained by collaborative relationships, and decisions were arrived at by use of consensus.

A *vision* was initially created by reaching consensus of the committee's membership on what it desired the school district to look like within 10 years of the present. Once the initial vision was reached, the committee decided that it must collect additional information and then determine whether its initial vision had to be somewhat modified when faced with this added information.

The first task of the committee was to reach agreement on its *beliefs and values*. Some of the beliefs and values agreed to by the committee members were

- All students can learn, whether they be N–12 or adult students.
- Schools should be seen as a part of a total community, and they should have important roles to play in society.
- Students, parents, citizens, and employees should all be thought of as customers, and they should be treated in a manner in which one would like to be treated oneself.
- Employees, students, parents, and citizens should be involved in the school district's decision-making process, and they should be a valuable source of feedback data on how well the school district is meeting its quality specifications.

- Not only should the school district be responsible for turning out highly productive citizens, but it also should be held responsible for providing high-quality services to all its customers.
- Planning is a necessary ingredient in achieving quality products and services, and this planning should be based on hard data (facts) and soft data (opinions and attitudes).
- All persons have equal worth, and each one should be treated as a most valuable commodity, to be cared for, valued, and nurtured to become the best that she or he can be.

Once the committee agreed upon its beliefs and values, it turned to its scanning tasks. Its *external scanning* indicated the following: (1) the community was becoming heavily multicultural; (2) many children lived in single-parent homes, and practically all of these single parents worked at least at one full-time job; (3) although state aid to the district appeared to be decreasing, new businesses were moving in to provide a much higher local tax base; and (4) the number of retired persons living within the school district continued to increase.

The *internal scanning* activities revealed that (1) the student dropout rate in the district's high school was in excess of 25%, and the rate displayed an increasing trend; (2) employees' attitudes remained positive for 96% of the employees; (3) school climate surveys revealed a decreasing trend in student-to-teacher, and student-to-principal, communication; and (4) there was a trend toward a decreasing number of applicants for teaching jobs, principalships, and skilled classified employees' positions.

After a great deal of discussion over two months of meetings, consensus was reached on the six Critical Success Factors (CSFs) that should draw the greatest attention from those who manage and operate the school district and that should gain the focus of most of the district's resources. The CSFs agreed upon were as follows:

1. *All* students should learn at their highest level of achievement in all their academic endeavors.
2. *All* students should graduate from high school and become productive citizens. A *productive citizen* is defined as one who produces more than she or he consumes.
3. Internal and external customer satisfaction is crucial.
4. The school district should provide continuingly higher quality in all its products and services.
5. Since the school district really belongs to the community at large, many stakeholders shall be directly involved in the decision making of the schools.
6. Strategic (long term, to achieve a vision) planning and tactical (the means or hows to achieve that vision) planning are obligatory continuing activities of the school district. Input, feedback, two-way communication, and recycling are integral parts of this planning.

Based upon this collection of information and upon the needs discovered by its assessment of mega (societal), macro (total school district), and micro (individual school) needs, the stakeholders' committee arrived at its *vision 2*. This modified the original vision to include (1) stress on community's involvement with the schools, (2) aspirations for high levels of achievement for all students, (3) continuous strategic and tactical planning, (4) the development of productive citizens, (5) the requirement to satisfy its internal and external customers, and (6) the desire to continuously improve the quality of the products and services developed by the schools and delivered to its internal and external customers.

Having arrived at its operationalized vision, the stakeholders' committee then approached the task of developing a one-sentence *mission statement*. The result is indicated below.

The *mission* of the Effective School District is to produce high-achieving and productive citizens and to provide continually improved products and services to all of its internal and external customers.

Once the mission statement had been agreed upon, the stakeholders' committee turned to the task of developing *strategic goals*. The goals that were accepted by the committee members and that fell within the structure of the vision and mission agreed upon are listed below:

- All students will be expected to learn at a mastery (80%) or higher level.
- Teachers, administrators, and students will all have high aspirations.
- Strong leadership in matters of instruction and management will be provided by teachers and administrators.
- A safe and orderly instructional climate will be maintained at all times.
- A respectful and caring attitude will be displayed to all internal and external customers of the schools.
- Data collection, two-way communication, and feedback for the purposes of improving academic achievement and the quality level of all services and products shall become an integral part of the normal operational procedures of the school district.
- The school district is a valued part of the total community, and parents, community members, and other important stakeholders shall be part of the communication, planning, feedback, and evaluation mechanism of the school district.
- Collaborative decision making shall be the process utilized, and it shall take place within a supportive climate.
- Most operational decisions shall be made at the school site level, and the authority and accountability related to many personnel, budgetary, governance, and instructional matters shall be made by an empowered committee of stakeholders who have a stake in the local schools' outcomes.
- Strategic and tactical planning shall be an integral part of the school district's standard operating procedures. Action programs shall spell out the means of achieving the goals.

- A value-added approach to constant striving for improved quality at each step of each activity shall be the norm.
- The final outcomes shall be well-educated, productive citizens, and the delivery of quality products and services to all of the school district's customers.

Having reached consensus on the strategic goals for which to strive, the committee turned to the task of analyzing the internal and external factors that might favorably or unfavorably affect the school district's ability to achieve the strategic goals. To accomplish this, a SWOT (strengths, weaknesses, opportunities, and threats) Analysis was used. The results of the SWOT Analysis indicated the probable factors to be in existence in the internal and external environments. Only two of each type will be provided here for the purpose of illustration.

Internal SWOT Analysis Findings

1. High employee morale will assist in achieving the goals (strength).
2. A high student dropout rate exists, and the trend indicates an increase (weakness).

External SWOT Analysis Findings

1. A large number of retired residents live within the school district, and they can be organized as volunteers, speakers for classes, and tutors for students (opportunity).
2. State aid for the school district has a declining pattern (threat).

Once the strategic goals were decided upon and the SWOT Analysis was completed, the stakeholders' committee addressed the *specific measurable objectives* that were to be attained in order to achieve each generally stated goal. Two examples of the numerous objectives upon which agreement was reached will suffice to demonstrate this step.

Objective 1: Within one year, the student dropout rate will be reduced by 5%; within five years, the student dropout rate will be less than 3%.

Objective 2: Within one year, a School-based Management committee will be operational within every school in the district; within five years, a minimum of 51% of all the residents of the community will have a direct and continuing role to play within the school district.

The stakeholders' committee discovered that they had too many goals to be achieved during the five-year period established for the initial strategic plan, and they also discovered that some goals had far too many specific objectives to be accomplished during the time frame allowed. Thus, the committee's members decided to develop a set of very pragmatic and simply worded decision rules to assist them in determining the highest-priority goals and the highest-priority objectives to be attempted during the five-year period. The three *decision rules* developed by the stakeholders' committee were

- The goal or objective must be *achievable.*
- The goal or objective must be *affordable.*
- The goal or objective must be *meaningful.*

Using the decision rules they had decided upon, the stakeholders' committee members turned the tactical planning process over to the administrators, teachers, and other school employees to develop specific action plans. However, the committee members recommended that the superintendent and other school employees provide a monthly progress report at the regularly scheduled school board meeting and that they meet quarterly with the stakeholders' committee to provide information and to receive feedback.

The employees began developing action plans by conducting four exercises: (1) brainstorming alternative action programs, (2) conducting a force-field analysis, (3) conducting a cost/benefit analysis, and (4) selecting the best alternative program based upon the three steps above.

Brainstorming was conducted using the following rules in order to achieve the greatest number of ideas in the shortest period of time (usually no longer than 10 minutes).

Brainstorming Rules

- All ideas are encouraged.
- There is to be no discussion of ideas.
- There is to be no explanation of the ideas presented.
- Piggybacking on another person's idea is legitimate.
- There is to be no verbal or nonverbal approval or disapproval of any idea.

An example of the brainstorming done by the tactical planners resulted in 85 ideas that they developed in seven minutes related to the best ways to get the community more involved with the schools.

Once they had reviewed the brainstorming ideas, they limited further deliberations to the two most promising ideas. At this point, they completed a force-field analysis, listing the supporting factors and the constraining factors for the promising idea of creating School-based Management committees at each local school building. An abbreviated example follows.

Force-field Analysis for Idea 1

Idea. School-based Management committees were to be organized at each school building, and the committee's membership was to include many representatives of parents, school booster groups, and the community. These members, along with representatives of teachers, classified employees, and the principal, were to be given wide decision-making authority related to the budget, personnel, instructional activities, and governance policies related to the local school's operation.

Supporting Factors

1. Teachers, parents, and citizens want more to say about how school is run.

2. This approach will bring much greater support for the school's programs.
3. This approach is being promoted across the United States.
4. Businesses are supportive of SBM.
5. Teachers' unions are supportive of this approach.
6. Other (specify).

Constraining Factors

1. The board of education and the superintendent are uneasy about delegating much of their decision-making authority.
2. Some principals are unwilling to share their decision-making power, and they are concerned about their accountability, which accompanies SBM.
3. Many teachers are unwilling to spend the additional time after normal school hours to implement SBM.
4. It is dangerous to provide decision-making power to a group whose members are not experienced in group decision making or accountability.
5. Other (specify).

Having analyzed the supports and constraints, the tactical planners decided to take the next step of completing a *cost/benefit analysis* of this idea. They found that the only financial costs involved would be those of training and the cost of coffee, snacks, and the typing of minutes of decisions that were reached. The total per year per building was estimated at $1,000, and the anticipated benefits were determined to far exceed the costs.

Finally, both of the ideas that had evolved during the initial brainstorming appeared to be promising and feasible, and the committee decided to implement them both.

Once the two action programs to be implemented were decided upon, the strategic planners developed a listing of tasks to be completed, timelines, persons responsible for completion of each task, and other important matters, utilizing the format displayed in Table 5.1.

TABLE 5.1 Detailed Action Plan Format

Tasks	Chronology	Person(s) Responsible	Time Target	Resources	Measures of Completion

After the action plans had been in operation, data were collected and analyzed, and decisions were made as to the degree of success experienced for each plan. This information was recycled to determine whether the action program would be (1) continued, (2) tried again with modifications, or (3) dropped and a different action program developed to attempt to achieve the objective. Whatever the final result, the information was returned to the strategic planning stakeholders' committee. The committee took the results of the tactical action plans and (1) reviewed its beliefs and values statements, (2) monitored its internal and external scanning data, (3) reviewed its CSFs, and (4) recycled the process to determine whether or not its vision, strategic goals, and specific objectives were still valid. At this stage the entire process was renewed for possible modifications.

Final Words

Many novel programs and means are suggested, from numerous internal and external sources, as restructuring ideas that will improve our schools and school districts. It is crucial that the local decision makers study these carefully for (1) their individual worth and potential for quality improvement in the schools and (2) their possibility of being integrated with other promising subsets of a holistic transformational and systemic change model designed to restructure and improve the quality of schools.

The keys to successfully implementing and maintaining a holistic transformational change are many, but the main ones include the following:

- Stakeholders must be involved in the process and in the decisions.
- Strategic and operational (tactical) plans must be identified and carried out by the decision makers and the managers of change, and these plans must be aligned.
- The vision, the goals, and the objectives that spell out the various levels of desired results must be clear and understood by all.
- Data must be collected and analyzed, and feedback must be provided to the decision makers and to the managers of change so that they can make improvements and modifications as required over time.
- Employees and a critical mass of other stakeholders must believe in the preferred future vision for the school district and its constituent schools, and they must accept ownership of the strategic goals, specific objectives, and tactical plans that are designed to achieve the preferred future vision.
- The preferred future vision must be one that includes continuous improvement of the quality of the products and services of the school district and its constituent schools. Once this result is attained, the district will witness a mass of satisfied internal and external customers.

What is suggested herein is not a quick fix or foolproof method of improving schools. It is, however, a long-term overview approach that integrates the various most popular current restructuring ideas into a holistic approach to school improvement. It avoids conflicts among the various suggested approaches, and it holds great promise for attaining the ultimate goals—turning out high-quality graduates who will become productive citizens and providing all of the schools' customers with high-quality services and products.

Annotated Bibliography

Quality References

Choppin, J. (1991). *Quality through people: A blueprint for proactive total quality management.* San Diego, CA: Pfeiffer.

Although this book is directed to the industrial sector, it presents examples that provide insights for educators. It provides a framework of ideas and theory that can be of assistance to those interested in initiating and improving their organization's approach to quality.

Herman, J. (1992). Total quality management basics: TQM comes to school. *School Business Affairs, 58*(4), 20-28.

This article reviews Deming's 14 points, relates some definitions to TQM from noted authors, and develops a series of models to display how the quality concepts can fit into the various major functions that are required to be performed in a high qualitative manner by school districts.

An introduction to total quality for schools. (1991). Arlington, VA: American Association of School Administrators.

This publication provides a series of 33 articles on W. Edwards Deming and the concepts of Total Quality Management.

Quality Digest. Red Bluff, CA: QCI International.

*This journal is published monthly, and it provides informa-
tion about the quality movement from the manufacturing
and service fields, including some information from the field
of education.*

Quality Progress. Milwaukee, WI: American Society for Quality
Control.

*This monthly journal provides a wide variety of informative
articles about the quality movement. On occasion, it devotes
an entire issue to information about quality in a specific
field. An example is the April 1992 issue, which is devoted
to quality issues in the field of health care.*

Scherkenbach, W. (1991). *The Deming route to quality and productivity: Road maps and roadblocks.* Washington, DC: George
Washington University, CEEP Press.

*Mr. Scherkenbach, who knows a great deal about W. Ed-
wards Deming's approach to quality, focuses the entire
volume on Deming's 14 points; he devotes a total chapter to
each of Deming's points.*

Effective Schools References

Brookover, W., Beamer, L., Efthim, H., Hathaway, D., Lezotte,
L., Miller, S., Passalacqua, J., & Tornatsky, L. (1982). *Creating effective schools: An inservice program for enhancing school
learning climate and achievement.* Holmes Beach, FL: Learning Publications.

*Wilbur Brookover and seven other authors who have been in
the forefront of the effective schools movement discuss such
topics as (1) an effective school learning climate, (2) expectations for learning, (3) effective instruction, (4) classroom
management, (5) team learning, (6) reinforcing achievement, and (7) use of assessment data for school achievement.
This is a must-read resource volume for anyone interested
in the effective schools movement.*

Levine, D. (1991). Creating effective schools: Findings and implications for research and practice. *Phi Delta Kappan, 72*(5), 389-393.

This article presents the conclusions reached by a 1990 report entitled: "Unusually Effective Schools: A Preview and Analysis of Research and Practice." Guidelines for multischool improvement projects are included.

Lezotte, L. *Effective schools research abstracts.* Okemos, MI: Effective Schools Products.

These abstracts are distributed monthly to subscribers, and they are organized within an annual three-ring notebook. Monthly updates are provided on any matter related to the effective school movement.

Newman, F., et al. (1991). *National Center on Effective Secondary Schools' final report on OERI Grant no. G-00869007.* Madison, WI: Wisconsin Center for Education Research.

This report presents a summary of the findings of six projects conducted by the National Center on Effective Secondary Schools.

School-based Management References

Herman, J. (1990). School-based management: A checklist of things to consider. *NASSP Bulletin, 74*(527), 67-71.

This article presents a series of items to be considered by individuals who are contemplating initiating the structure and process of School-based Management. The information is presented in an easily used checklist format.

Herman, J. J., & Herman, J. L. (in press). *School-based management: Current thinking and practice.* Springfield, IL: Charles C. Thomas.

This book is a comprehensive presentation of the current state of School-based Management in the United States. It also provides a summary of the most thorough mandated state legislation approach to this restructuring scheme—

*that of the Kentucky Reform Act of 1990—and it pre-
sents the results of a series of initial perceptions toward
implementation of this act by some of the local committee
members who are participants in a county school district in
Kentucky.*

Lane, J., & Epps, E. (Eds.). (1992). *Restructuring the schools:
Problems and prospects.* Berkeley, CA: McCutchan.

*Although this volume provides an overview of the restruc-
turing movement in schools, it primarily focuses on the
topic of School-based Management. It provides information
about School-based Management initiatives in Chicago,
Cincinnati, and South Carolina. It also discusses important
policy issues related to School-based Management.*

Lewis, J., Jr. (1989). *Implementing school-based management by
empowering teachers.* Westbury, NY: J. L. Wilkerson.

*This volume presents down-to-basics, practical information
that details the history of School-based Management, defines the roles of participants, suggests implementation procedures, describes the role of the principal in a School-based
Management structure, identifies implementation training
needs, presents means of evaluating School-based Management, and details the factors that limit School-based
Management.*

School-based management: Theory and practice. (1991). Reston, VA:
National Association of Secondary School Principals.

*This monograph presents 17 articles dealing with various
aspects of School-based Management.*

Strategic and Tactical Planning References

Bryson, J. (1988). *Strategic planning for public and nonprofit organizations: A guide to strengthening and sustaining organizational achievement.* San Francisco: Jossey-Bass.

*The author stresses the need to understand the dynamics of
strategic planning, the key steps in thinking and acting
strategically, and the means of successfully implementing*

strategic planning. Included in the text is a series of resource worksheets and sample strategies.

Carlson, R., & Awkerman, G. (Eds.). (1991). *Educational planning: Concepts, strategies, practices.* New York: Longman.

Twenty-three authors provide theoretical underpinnings, policy analyses, strategic planning concepts, operational planning concepts, and case study materials.

Herman, J. (1992). Strategic Planning: Reasons for failed attempts. *Educational Planning, 8*(3), 36-40.

Emphasis is placed on the reasons why strategic planning attempts have failed, with the intention of alerting planners of items to avoid in order to keep their strategic plans positive and on target.

Kaufman, R., & Herman, J. (1991). *Strategic planning in education: Rethinking, restructuring, revitalizing.* Lancaster, PA: Technomic.

This is a comprehensive volume discussing and illustrating, with practical examples and exercises, all the important concepts involved in strategic planning. It also provides how-to information about each step of the strategic planning process, beginning with creating a preferred future vision and ending with means of evaluating the formative and summative results achieved.

Morrisey, G., Below, P., & Acomb, B. (1987). *The executive guide to operational planning.* San Francisco: Jossey-Bass.

This book deals with the means to accomplish the desired goals and tasks. It provides information about such matters as (1) developing an operational analysis, (2) determining key indicators of performance, (3) selecting operating objectives, (4) preparing operational plans, and (5) integrating budgets with the plans.